The Story of

Remembrance Day

Monica Hughes

www.raintreepublishers.co.uk
Visit our website to find out more information about **Raintree** books.

To order:
☎ Phone 44 (0) 1865 888112
📄 Send a fax to 44 (0) 1865 314091
💻 Visit the Raintree Bookshop at **www.raintreepublishers.co.uk** to browse our catalogue and order online.

First published in Great Britain by Raintree, Halley Court, Jordan Hill, Oxford OX2 8EJ, part of Pearson Education. Raintree is a registered trademark of Pearson Education Ltd.

Editorial: Sian Smith
Design: Kimberley R. Miracle, Big Top and
   Joanna Hinton-Malivoire
Picture research: Ruth Blair
Production: Duncan Gilbert
Illustrated by Beehive Illustration
Originated by Dot Gradations

Printed and bound in China by Leo Paper Group

ISBN 978 1 4062 1013 2 (hardback)
ISBN 978 1 4062 1023 1 (paperback)

12 11 10 09 08
10 9 8 7 6 5 4 3 2 1

British Library Cataloguing in Publication Data
 Hughes, Monica
   The story of Remembrance Day
1. Remembrance Sunday - Juvenile literature
2. Armistice Day - Juvenile literature
   I. Title

940.4'6

Acknowledgments
The publishers would like to thank the following for permission to reproduce photographs: ©Alamy pp. 13 (Brian Harris Editorial Photographer), 17 (David Burges), 18 (David hancock),19 (Enigma), 4 (Martin Norris), 16 (Michael Jenner), 14 (Paul David Drabble), 9 (Roger Bamber), 5 (Stan Kujawa), 7 (The National Trust Photolibrary), 15 (67photo); ©The Art Archive p.6 (Imperial War Museum); ©Corbis p. 11 (Bettmann); ©Getty Images pp.10 (Hulton Archive),8, 12 (News); ©istockphoto.com p.; ©National Archives & Records Administration pp.14 (top left), 14 (bottom left), 14 (bottom right), 15 (top left), 15 (top right), 15 (bottom left), 15 (bottom right); ©The Illustrated London News Picture Library p.15

Cover photograph reproduced with permission of ©Corbis (Reuters, Dylan Martinez)

Every effort has been made to contact copyright holders of any material reproduced in this book. Any omissions will be rectified in subsequent printings if notice is given to the publisher.

Contents

Some words are printed in bold, **like this**. You can find out what they mean in the glossary.

Symbols of remembrance

This wreath of poppies is a symbol of remembrance.

In November you will see people selling and wearing poppies. You may see **wreaths** of poppies on **war memorials**. You might see **veterans** wearing medals and marching behind flags.

These are all **symbols** of remembrance. The symbols help us remember the people who have died in wars.

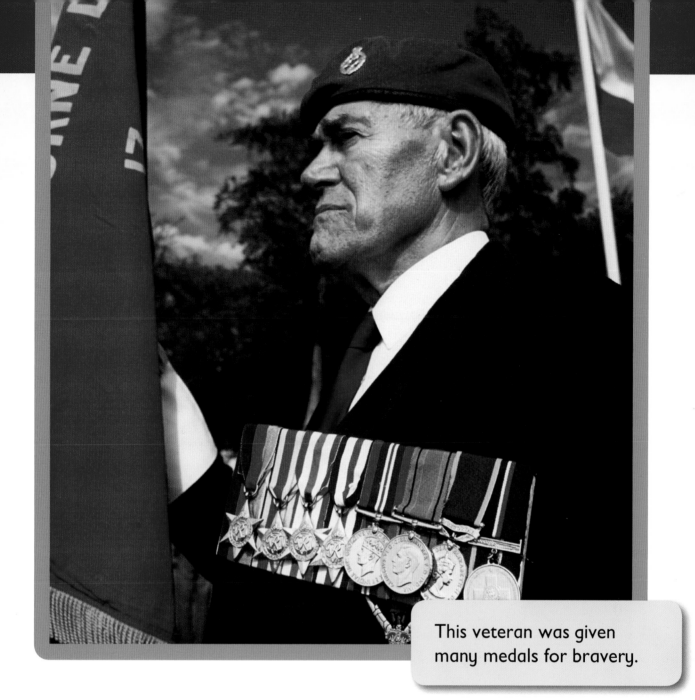

This veteran was given many medals for bravery.

We remember their bravery and that they died so we can be free. The symbols also remind us of the **servicemen** and women who have been hurt. We remember the people who are still suffering today because of war, such as children who have lost their home or their family.

Why poppies for remembrance?

Soldiers in a trench during the First World War.

The First World War lasted for four years. Millions of soldiers were killed and many more were hurt. The soldiers fought from **trenches** that were dug into the ground across the battlefields. Everywhere houses, farms, and trees were destroyed.

The battlefields turned into a sea of wet mud each winter. When warm weather came the only plants to grow in the dried earth were red poppies. The poppies reminded the soldiers of their friends who had died. The poppies became a **symbol** of hope to those who were still fighting.

The first poppies

The different parts of these artificial poppies have to be put together.

The first poppies were worn in 1918. They were real flowers. People wore them to remember those who had recently died in the war. Later, **artificial** poppies were made by **disabled veterans** and sold to help ex-**servicemen** and their families.

Making poppies at the British Legion factory in Richmond.

Today the **British Legion** poppy factory makes poppies and **wreaths** all year round. Many of the people who make the poppies are disabled. Poppies are sold from mid-October until Remembrance Sunday in November. The money raised goes to help servicemen and women and their families.

The first Remembrance Day

Men who signed the Armistice, outside the railway carriage where it was signed.

The first Remembrance Day was called **Armistice** Day. The First World War ended with the signing of the Armistice in a railway carriage in 1918. The fighting stopped at exactly 11 o'clock on 11 November, or at the eleventh hour of the eleventh day of the eleventh month.

The two minutes' silence on Armistice day in 1925.

From 1919 to 1945 Armistice Day was celebrated every 11 November. Men, women, and children stood in silence for two minutes at 11 o'clock in remembrance. This two minutes' silence still takes place today.

Remembrance Sunday

Wreaths placed at the Cenotaph on Remembrance Sunday.

The Sunday nearest to 11 November is now a special day where we honour those killed and injured in wars. We remember the soldiers killed in both world wars and other more recent **conflicts** like those in the South Atlantic and Iraq.

The Last Post being played.

A large ceremony is held at the **Cenotaph** in London on Remembrance Sunday. **Wreaths** of poppies are laid. **Servicemen** and women march past wearing their uniforms and medals. A **bugler** plays the Last Post and there is a two minutes' silence. Similar ceremonies are held at **war memorials** throughout the country.

Who do we remember?

We remember those who died in the First and Second World War. We remember people who suffered during these wars and in other wars in the past. We think about wars and **conflicts** today, the people who have died, and the people who are still in danger.

We remember the injured **servicemen** and **servicewomen** still being looked after. **Civilians** who helped in wartime are remembered. We also think about the children who have lost parents and people whose homes have been destroyed.

War memorials

Memorial to women killed in the Second World War.

There are **war memorials** all over this country and in other parts of the world. There are different types including **plaques**, statues, stone columns, and special gates. Some were put up to remember those who died in both world wars.

Part of the stone circle memorial in Staffordshire.

Other memorials remind us of those killed more recently. In 2007 a memorial stone circle was built in Staffordshire. It was built to honour all those killed in **conflicts** since the end of the Second World War.

A new memorial has also been built in London to remember the animals that have died or suffered in wars.

Remembrance Day around the world

Veterans Day in America.

In both world wars soldiers and **civilians** from as far away as India, Africa, Australia, and New Zealand were killed and injured.

In America all those who served their country in war are remembered on 11 November. This day is known as **Veterans'** Day.

In Australia and New Zealand ANZAC day is held on 25 April. On that day those who died are remembered and the people who returned from the wars are honoured.

People from all over the world have suffered because of wars. Having special days for remembrance helps us to make sure that these people and the things that happened are not forgotten.

ANZAC Day in Australia.

Teachers' guide

These books have followed the QCA guidelines closely, but space has not allowed us to cover all the information and vocabulary the QCA suggest. Any suggested material not covered in the book is added to the discussion points below. The books can simply be read as information books, or they could be used as a focus for studying the unit. Below are discussion points grouped in pairs of pages, with suggested follow-up activities.

PAGES 4–5

Talk about:
- Wearing poppies and one day a year as a special 'remembering' day. What other one-day-a-year events can they think of? (These will probably include religious days like Christmas and personal special days like family birthdays and anniversaries). Explain that, just as it is important not to forget their birthday, when Remembrance Day was set up (in 1918, at the end of the First World War) it was seen as important not to forget all the people who died.

Possible activity:
- Make a list of yearly 'days' under the heading of religious days, personal special days, other special days.

PAGES 6–7

Talk about:
- The First World War and its huge levels of casualties. It began in August 1914 and people were expecting it to be over by Christmas – it ended on 11 November 1918, when the Germans asked for an Armistice: a stopping of the war to negotiate peace. Almost every family in Britain lost at least one family member. Some women lost a husband one or more brothers and one or more sons.

Possible activity:
- Read and discuss the poem "In Flanders Fields ...", which can be found at the bottom of the webpage http://www.firstworldwar.com/poetsandprose/inflandersfields.htm. The language is hard, but the feeling of the poem comes over in reading it.

PAGES 8–9

Talk about:
- Explain about wearing poppies. Discuss why people would want to wear a poppy to show everyone, even strangers in the street, what they feel. Discuss white poppies. These were worn from 1933 onwards, by people who wanted to remember those who died but did not approve of war and felt that the traditional red poppies showed approval of war, as well as remembering the dead.

Possible activity:
- Collect and display a variety of charity pins and badges.

PAGES 10–11

Talk about:
- The two minute silence on the eleventh hour of the eleventh day in November. Why is it more powerful if everyone is still and quiet at the same time? Explain that Remembrance Day is not now always 11 November – it is the nearest Sunday to it. Why a Sunday? Why change from the exact day (what problems can they think of at work, in school etc).

Possible activity:
- Set the timer and stand absolutely still and quiet for two minutes.

PAGES 12–13

Talk about:

• What happens on Remembrance Sunday; that we are remembering those killed in all the wars right through to the present day. The ceremony at the Cenotaph in London and what happens there. The fact that it happens all over Britain. Where is the closest place to your school where there is a ceremony?

Possible activity:

• Listen to the Last Post. It can be found as an MP3 download at http://www.banquetmusic.co.uk/ bugler.html?gclid=CNaN19rPrZlCFQo2Qwodmz-zQQ.

PAGES 14–15

Talk about:

• How everyone can do their own kind of remembering. How after the First World War people were remembering the dead of that war but that, as time has gone on and there have been more wars, different people do different kinds of remembering. Some people remember family. Some people remember the soldiers who fought and died, other people remember civilians who died.

Possible activity:

• Ask relatives or neighbours who they remember. Bring at least one coloured circle to school that says 'My Mum/gran/neighbour remembers... because...' for a remembrance display.

PAGES 16–17

Talk about:

• Discuss the fact that war memorials come in many different shapes and sizes. Discuss the pictures in the book on pages 16 and 17. A Google images search on 'war memorial' will bring up many more. They are very different but most have the names of the local war dead on them.

Possible activity:

• War memorial visit (see **Local history work** below).

PAGES 18–19

Talk about:

• Discuss the different names for days for remembering those who died in wars in different countries and the fact that some places give the day a different name. Sometimes this can be confusing. In the USA they celebrate Veterans' Day on 11 November. However, this day celebrates all those who have ever fought for the country and is mainly to honour living soldiers and ex-soldiers. Their day for remembering the dead is Memorial Day, 25 May.

Possible activity:

• Design a poster to celebrate Remembrance Day.

Local history work

Most schools have a war memorial within walking distance. QCA suggest a visit to your local war memorial, to discuss exactly what is on it, how many people died in each war and why and when it was built. We would also suggest the possibility of local surnames carrying through to the Second World War from the First World War as a thing to look for.

Find out more

Books

Beginning History: Remembrance Day,
Liz Gogerly (Hodder Wayland, 2003)

Don't Forget: Remembrance Day,
Monica Hughes (Heinemann Library, 2003)

World at War – World War II: Children During Wartime,
Brian Williams (Heinemann Library, 2007)

Websites

www.bbc.co.uk/religion/remembrance/veterans/
You can read and hear interviews with veterans from World War I on this site.

www.ukstudentife.com/Ideas/Album/RemembranceSunday.htm
This site has photos taken at the cenotaph in London during a Remembrance Day ceremony.

Places to visit

The Cenotaph in Whitehall, London.

War memorials in your own town or city.

Glossary

armistice agreement to stop fighting

artificial something made to look like the real thing

British Legion charity helping veterans and their families

bugler someone who plays a bugle, which is like a small trumpet

Cenotaph war memorial in London. You can see a photo of this on page 11.

civilian not a serviceman or woman

conflict fight or battle

disabled when someone cannot use their body properly because it has been injured

plaque a metal plate with writing on it, fixed to a wall

servicemen/servicewomen soldiers

symbol something that has a special meaning

trench long deep hole dug in the ground

veteran experienced serviceman or woman

war memorial something built to help us remember people who died or suffered in wars

wreath flowers joined together to make a circle

Index